Baseball

Written by Elizabeth Apgar
Photographs by John Paul Endress

Get a bag.

Get a hat.

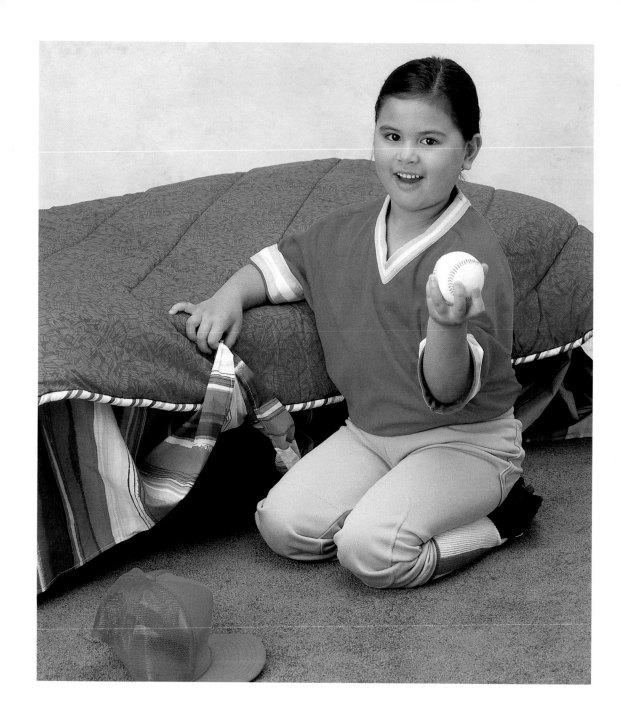

Get a ball.

Get a bat.

Get a bike.

Baseball!

This

Ladybird First Favourite Tale

belongs to

....

Published by Ladybird Books Ltd
A Penguin Company
Penguin Books Ltd, 80 Strand, London WC2R 0RL, UK
Penguin Books Australia Ltd, Camberwell, Victoria, Australia
Penguin Group (NZ) 67 Apollo Drive, Rosedale, North Shore 0632, New Zealand

001 – 10 9 8 7 6 5 4 3 2 1

© Ladybird Books Ltd MCMXCIX
This edition MMXII

ISBN: 978-1-40930-956-7

Printed in China

Ladybird First Favourite Tales

Chicken Licken

BASED ON A TRADITIONAL FOLK TALE
retold by Mandy Ross ★ illustrated by Sam Childs

Chicken Licken is minding his chicken-pecking business one day, when an acorn drops – PLOP! on his head.

"Help!" he cheeps. "The sky is falling down! I'd better go and tell the king."

And off he scurries.
"What's the hurry?" clucks . . .

. . . Henny Penny.

"Oh, Henny Penny!" cheeps Chicken Licken.
"The sky is falling down! I'm off to tell
the king."

"That's not funny!" clucks Henny Penny.
"I'd better come, too."

It's a terrible tale!

. . . Cocky Locky.

"Oh, Cocky Locky!" cheeps Chicken Licken. "The sky is falling down! We're off to tell the king."

"What a cock-a-doodle shock!" crows Cocky Locky. "I'd better come, too."

The king must know!

So Chicken Licken, Henny Penny and Cocky Locky scurry along to tell the king.

"What's the hurry?" quack . . .

"Oh, Ducky Lucky and Drakey Lakey!" cheeps Chicken Licken. "The sky is falling down! We're off to tell the king."

"You look very shaky!" quacks Drakey Lakey. "We'd better come, too."

So Chicken Licken, Henny Penny, Cocky Locky, Ducky Lucky and Drakey Lakey scurry along to tell the king.

"What's the hurry?" honks ...

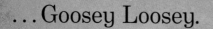. . . Goosey Loosey.

"Oh, Goosey Loosey!" cheeps Chicken Licken. "The sky is falling down! We're off to tell the king."

"Goodness gracious!" gasps Goosey Loosey. "I'd better come, too."

"Oh, Turkey Lurkey!" cheeps Chicken Licken. "The sky is falling down! We're off to tell the king."

"I feel horribly wobbly," gobbles Turkey Lurkey. "I'd better come, too."

So Chicken Licken, Henny Penny,
Cocky Locky, Ducky Lucky, Drakey Lakey,
Goosey Loosey and Turkey Lurkey scurry
along to tell the king.

"What's the hurry?" snaps . . .

"Oh, Foxy Loxy!" cheeps Chicken Licken. "The sky is falling down! We're off to tell the king."

"Aha!" smiles Foxy Loxy. He has a cunning plan.

"Follow me, my feathery friends," smiles
Foxy Loxy. "I can help you find the king."

So Chicken Licken, Henny Penny,
Cocky Locky, Ducky Lucky,
Drakey Lakey, Goosey Loosey and
Turkey Lurkey hurry and scurry
behind Foxy Loxy, all the way to . . .

...the Foxy Loxy family lair – just in time for dinner.

And that was the end of Chicken Licken,
Henny Penny, Cocky Locky, Ducky Lucky,
Drakey Lakey, Goosey Loosey and
Turkey Lurkey.

And the king never did find out that the sky
was falling down.